NEW VANGUARD 245

EARLY US ARMOR

Tanks 1916–40

STEVEN J. ZALOGA   ILLUSTRATED BY FELIPE RODRIGUEZ

First published in Great Britain in 2017 by Osprey Publishing,
PO Box 883, Oxford, OX1 9PL, UK
1385 Broadway, 5th Floor, New York, NY 10018, USA
E-mail: info@ospreypublishing.com

Osprey Publishing, part of Bloomsbury Publishing Plc

A CIP catalog record for this book is available from the British Library

Print ISBN: 978 1 47281 807 2
PDF e-book ISBN: 978 1 47281 808 9
ePub e-book ISBN: 978 1 47281 809 6

Index by Sandra Shotter
Typeset in Sabon and Myriad Pro
Originated by PDQ Media, Bungay, UK
Printed in China through World Print Ltd.

17 18 19 20 21 10 9 8 7 6 5 4 3 2

Osprey Publishing supports the Woodland Trust, the UK's leading woodland
conservation charity. Between 2014 and 2018 our donations are being
spent on their Centenary Woods project in the UK.

To find out more about our authors and books visit
www.ospreypublishing.com. Here you will find extracts, author
interviews, details of forthcoming events and the option to sign up for
our newsletter.

PHOTOS

Unless otherwise specified, all photos are from the author's collection.

COVER IMAGE

M2A3 at the Annual Army Day Parade in Washington, 1939 (Courtesy of the
Library of Congress, LC-DIG-hec-26434)

CONTENTS

EARLY US ARMOR

TANKS 1916–40

AMERICAN TANK ORIGINS

Prior to World War II, the US Army procured fewer tanks than most of the major and minor armies of Europe. Yet in World War II, the United States manufactured more armored combat vehicles than any other country. This book examines the early roots of American tank development in the years prior to World War II.

There are many legends about the early origins of American tanks, including the tale of a primitive vehicle protected by cotton bales that was used in the attack on Fort Hill during the Vicksburg campaign in the Civil War in 1863. The US Army began acquiring armored cars late in the 19th century, but showed little interest in tracked combat vehicles until its entry into World War I in 1917.

Early efforts in tank design were connected to America's prosperous tractor industry. Companies such as Holt Caterpillar and C. L. Best manufactured a wide range of tractors for industrial and agricultural use. As the war in Europe coagulated into muddy trench warfare, European armies began to buy more and more tractors from the United States. American

The 1917 Holt Gas-Electric Tank was armed with a 75mm mountain gun in the bow and a water-cooled .30cal machine gun in sponsons on either side.

The CLB 75 Tracklayer was one of the best known of the wartime parade tanks, and took part in civic activities in the San Francisco area. Built on a C. L. Best tractor, it is seen here taking part in a mock attack with troops of the California National Guard in 1918.

tractors were instrumental in early European tank designs since they were at the forefront of track and tractor technology.

A number of enterprising American firms tried to drum up European business by offering armored tractors. Edwin Wheelock, general manager of the Pioneer Tractor Company of Winona, Minnesota, claimed to have supplied the British War Office with plans for a 25-ton armored tractor in April 1915 some months before the first British efforts to develop a tank. Whether this unsolicited proposal had any influence on the British tank program is unrecorded, though Wheelock later claimed that it did. The Automatic Machine Company of Bridgeport, Connecticut proposed an Automatic Land Cruiser armed with a 1-pdr and machine guns to the British War Office and the French war ministry in July–August 1915. The Oakland Motor Company constructed the "Victoria tank" in December 1915 based on a British requirement. Although not accepted for production, the vehicle appeared at War Bond drives around the United States.

Most early American tank designs came after the first British use of tanks in 1916. In most cases, these were simply tractors with sheet-metal structures for patriotic parades. One of the best-known "tanks" of this period was a G-9 Caterpillar Tank built as a movie prop for the 1917 William Randolph Hearst movie *Patria* that promoted military preparedness for the United States. The C. L. Best Tractor Company of San Leandro, California built at least two parade tanks. One of these, the CLB 75 Tracklayer, was widely photographed at the 4th of July parade in 1917 in San Francisco and later took part in exercises with the California National Guard.

The first serious tank completed in the United States was the Holt Gas-Electric tank, a collaboration of Holt Caterpillar and the General Electric Company, in 1917–18. It was based on a modified Holt 75 tractor and powered by a Holt 90hp gasoline motor linked to a GE generator that powered an electric motor on each of the bogies. The largest and most

"War-Tank America" was built at MIT outside Boston in 1918 and powered by Doble steam engines. It was armed with a flamethrower and was demonstrated to the AEF in France late in 1918.

sophisticated tank built in the United States during the war was a collaboration of the US Army Corps of Engineers and the Massachusetts Institute of Technology (MIT). Maj Henry Adams of the Corps of Engineers developed a long-range flamethrower that used a steam boiler to atomize and propel a stream of fuel oil about 90 yards. It was successfully demonstrated in November 1917, leading to a scheme to mount the device in a steam-powered tank as a weapon to attack German pillboxes. "War Tank America," also known as the "Steam Tank," was patterned on British rhomboid tank designs and was powered by a pair of Doble steam engines offering 500hp. It was designed by Professor E. F. Miller, head of the MIT mechanical engineering department, and built at MIT in Cambridge under the direction of several Army officers. The Flame Projector, Tractor Type, Mark I was mounted in the front of the tank and there were sponsons on either side for .30cal machine guns. The Army did not have sufficient funds for the project, and it was built at a cost of $60,000 from the donations of Boston bankers. "War Tank America" weighed some 45 tons and it was completed in early 1918. In September 1918, it was dispatched to France and demonstrated to Gen John Pershing, the commander of the American Expeditionary Force (AEF), near his headquarters at Chaumont. It arrived too late to take part in any military actions.

One of the few early tanks to receive US Army funding was the so-called "Skeleton Tank" built by the Pioneer Tractor Company at a cost of about $15,000. The idea was to combine the light weight of the Renault FT tank with the trench-crossing ability of the larger British designs. To cut down on costs, much of the structure was made from ordinary iron pipes, and some of the suspension elements were made of wood. Besides cutting down on weight, the Skeleton Tank was designed to be shipped to France as a knocked-down kit to be assembled once it arrived. The armored module in the center contained two Beaver 50hp engines and a crew of two. The completed tank weighed 8 tons and it had a cross-country speed of 5mph. By the time the Skeleton Tank was ready, however, the war was over.

In 1918, the British war ministry approached several American automotive firms about a requirement for 22,000 Newton Tractors, an unarmored cross-country supply vehicle with a tracked suspension intended for the 1919 campaign. Studebaker used one of their examples as the basis for a small tank with two small machine-gun turrets on the roof.

THE TANK CORPS

The American entry into World War I in April 1917 accelerated US Army interest in obtaining tanks. A board of officers of the AEF submitted a report in late summer that indicated that a force of 20 divisions would require five heavy and 20 light tank battalions, totaling 375 heavy and

The Skeleton Tank was an attempt by the Pioneer Tractor Company to achieve the trench-crossing ability of the British rhomboid tanks with the lighter weight of the French Renault FT. The single prototype was displayed for many years at Aberdeen Proving Ground.

1,500 light tanks. Since there were no mature tank designs in the United States, the Ordnance Department turned to existing French and British designs.

In December 1917, a French Renault FT light tank arrived in the United States along with manufacturing drawings. To keep the cost low, Ordnance decided to adapt the design from metric measurements and to use an existing US-manufactured Buda engine. In February 1918, the War Department informed the AEF headquarters that they could expect to receive 100 American-built Six-Ton tanks in April, 300 in May, and 600 per month in subsequent months. This estimate proved wildly optimistic. Contracts were issued to three Ohio plants for 4,440 tanks at an average cost of $11,500 each. Production was centered at the Van Dorn Iron Works of Cleveland, and the Maxwell Motors Company and C. L. Best Company, both in Dayton. The first tanks were completed in October 1918, and by the time of the

A Renault FT commanded by Sgt O. F. Johnson of B Company, 2nd Platoon, 345th Tank Battalion, 1st Tank Brigade AEF in a repair area near Varennes-en-Argonne on October 12, 1918. By this stage of the Argonne campaign, the brigade's two battalions had been reduced to only a single Provisional Company with 24 tanks, which was organized at Varennes that day to support the next offensive on October 14. This particular Renault FT is fitted with an "Omnibus" plate turret with 37mm gun, while the two in the background have the Girod cast turret.

armistice on 11 November, 64 tanks were ready. The first two tanks arrived at the Langres tank school in France on 20 November 1918, followed by eight more in December, and so they never saw combat. Eventually some 952 Six-Ton tanks were completed, consisting of 372 gun tanks, 526 machine-gun tanks and 50 radio command tanks.

In the meantime, work was under way on the manufacture of the Mark VIII heavy tank, variously nicknamed the "International tank" or the "Liberty tank," the later name stemming from its use of the Liberty aircraft engine. The head of Britain's Mechanical Warfare Department, Lt Col Albert Stern, had suggested a joint US-UK-France collaborative effort based on a British design. A plan for a joint UK-USA assembly effort envisioned a

A

1: RENAULT FT, 2ND PLATOON, C COMPANY, 344TH TANK BATTALION, 304TH TANK BRIGADE, AEF, FRANCE 1918

This particular Char canon Renault FT had the Renault factory number 1516 painted in red on the hull side and the army registration number 67636 on the chassis frame. The Renault-manufactured FT tanks had company numbers in the 1 to 2000 range then 9001 to 9770 in the final batches. Renault was assigned a block of military registration numbers from 66000 to 68000. The AEF units left the tanks in their original French camouflage colors, in this case, the 1918 four-color Renault factory scheme of sand, green, brown, and black.

The AEF tank battalions followed the French practice of using playing card symbols to identify sub-formations. If French practice was followed, the first battalion of the brigade (326th/344th) would have used blue and second red (327th/345th), which is the pattern shown here. Charles Lemons in his book suggests that the colors used instead were a reddish brown and green. To further confuse matters, the preserved example of this tank at the Fort Meade museum shows the heart marking in red. The unit marking style was a circle for Company A, square for Company B and a triangle or diamond for Company C. The 1st Platoon used a spade, the 2nd a heart and the 3rd a diamond. The individual tanks within the platoon had a white number painted to the upper left of the marking. By the time of the October 4, 1918 fighting when in support of the 16th Infantry Regiment, the "Five of Hearts" was one of only two surviving tanks in the company. It was commanded by the platoon leader, Lt Wood, while the other was commanded by Sgt Arthur Snyder. When Wood was wounded and Snyder's tank was disabled at the start of the day's fighting, Snyder took over "Five of Hearts" along with a driver from the 345th. The tank fought for the remainder of the day, knocking out several German machine-gun nests and at least one field gun before finally being stopped after both crewmen were wounded. By this stage, the tank had been hit about a hundred times, and soldiers who recovered the tank described the interior as being "splattered with blood" from the two commanders and three drivers who had served in it and been wounded during the course of the day's fighting. The tank was recovered and sent back to Camp Meade after the war, and it is currently preserved in the post museum in Maryland.

2: SIX-TON TANK M1917, 26TH TANK COMPANY, 26TH YANKEE DIVISION (NATIONAL GUARD), BOSTON, MASSACHUSETTS, 1925

US-manufactured vehicles during World War I were painted in overall olive drab, though the shade was lighter than the postwar color, somewhat in the direction of the later Field Drab color. There was some use of elaborate multicolor camouflage schemes developed by the 40th Engineers in 1918 based on French influences and issued by Ordnance on October 15, 1918 as "Painting Instruction for Camouflaging of Ordnance Vehicles." The French Army itself conducted camouflage experiments in 1918 that indicated that an overall dark color was more effective camouflage than elaborate multicolor schemes and so standardized on a very dark green called army green (*vert armée*). The US Army followed suit after the war, adopting a new and darker shade of olive drab under US Army Specification 3-1. This was mixed from raw umber and black pigment, so the color was neither green nor brown, but a very dark mud color. Although Army regulations called for the use of lusterless paint on tactical vehicles, the practice was usually to use gloss paint or apply gloss varnish over the lusterless paint for a "spit 'n' polish" finish. Unit markings practices in the 1920s varied from unit to unit, and in the case of this National Guard tank company, the markings were limited to the tricolor triangle adopted by the Tank Corps during the war, plus a white vehicle number.

1

2

A Six-Ton tank M1917 armed with the 37mm gun M1916 in the late mount from A Company, 1st Tank Regiment attached to the Mechanized Force at Fort Eustis, Virginia, in August 1931.

scheme under which the tanks would be jointly manufactured, with final assembly of the British and American components taking place at a facility near the front lines in France. A formal agreement was signed in London on 19 January 1918 with an aim to manufacture 300 tanks per month with an eventual objective of reaching as many as 1,500 tanks monthly by the end of 1918. The price per tank was pegged at £5,000 or $35,000. The United States provided the engine, powertrain and running gear, costing about $15,000 per tank, while British plants would provide the armor and armament. The Anglo-American Commission established the final assembly plant at Neuvy-Pailloux, south of Paris. The first mild steel hull was completed by the North British Locomotive Company in Glasgow and shipped to the United States in July 1918 for installation of American components. This prototype was completed on 29 September 1918 and began testing in October 1918. By the time of the armistice, some 100 tank kits had been completed in Britain, along with seven complete tanks. The various US plants had completed about 700 sets of parts by the time of the armistice. The US Army agreed to purchase the 100 kits from Britain and they were eventually shipped to the Rock Island Arsenal where final assembly was completed in January–June 1920.

While these programs were under way, Ordnance held meetings with Ford Motor Company in the hopes of manufacturing tanks using existing automotive facilities. Ford began work on two separate designs, the small Three-Ton Special Tractor, and the larger Mark I tank. The Three-Ton was

The 301st Tank Battalion AEF was equipped with the British Mark V heavy tank. This was one of the Mark Vs sent back to the United States after the war and is seen during training at Camp Meade, Maryland, in the early 1920s.

a turretless tankette with a two-man crew and a single machine gun. It was powered by two Model T automobile engines that gave it a top speed of up to 8mph, which was considered quite speedy for the time. The Three-Ton was expected to cost only $4,000 each, and a contract was issued for 15,000 tanks with production expected to reach 100 per day by early 1919. A test batch of 15 tanks arrived in France shortly before the end of the war. The AEF Tank Corps in France was not at all enthused about the little tank, however,

The Ford Three-Ton tank proved to be too small to be practical, and of the thousands planned, only 15 were built.

and recommended that it be converted instead into an unarmed artillery tractor. In the event, only the first test batch of 15 tanks was ever completed and the contracts were canceled.

The Ford Mark I tank was essentially a redesigned and improved Renault FT better suited to mass production in the United States. Ford was awarded a contract for 1,000 tanks but only a single prototype was completed after the armistice. The contract was canceled along with plans for a Ford-built copy of the Renault FT with Hudson 60hp motor called the Mark II.

The inevitable delays in manufacturing tanks in the United States made the AEF entirely dependent on tanks obtained from Britain and France. France agreed to provide the Renault FT for light tank battalions and Britain agreed to provide the Mark V heavy tank. The French Army established a light tank school at Bourg/Langres. The French Army agreed to provide enough tanks for two battalions, starting with the loan of 25 Renault FT tanks in March–June 1918 for the training center. The first

A pair of Six-Ton tank M1917s with a Mark V tank behind them are seen at the "Panorama of Victory" display, part of a Victory Loan drive in Van Cortlandt Park, New York, on April 29, 1919. These show the early configuration of the Marlin machine-gun mount. The Six-Ton tank can be easily distinguished from the Renault FT since the muffler was located on the left hull side, not the right.

A pair of massive Mark VIII heavy tanks on exercise at Camp Meade, Maryland, in the early 1920s.

During the 1920s, 110 Six-Ton tanks were assigned to the tank companies of the National Guard. This is the divisional company of the 26th Yankee Division (NG) station in the Boston area. Tank 9 is a radio command tank while Tank 6 is armed with the 37mm gun. The remainder of the tanks are armed with the Browning .30cal machine gun in the later-style ball mount.

combat tanks were delivered in three batches between August 21 and September 2, 1918 and consisted of 45 tanks with machine guns and 30 tanks with 37mm guns. Led by Lt Col George S. Patton Jr, the new 326th (later 344th) and 327th (345th) battalions were first blooded in the fighting near St Mihiel on September 12, 1918. Their real trial-by-fire came later in the month during the Meuse-Argonne Forest battles, which began on September 26 and dragged on through November 1, 1918. Total combat losses were three Renaults in October and 29 in November 1918. In total, the AEF received 144 Renault FT combat tanks in August–September, one in October and 69 in December for a total of 214, not counting the 25 training tanks. A total of 213 Renault FT tanks were sent back to the United States after the war.

Britain provided 47 Mark V tanks to the 301st Tank Battalion by October 1918 and 12 more after the war. The Mark V and Mark V* first went into combat in the assault on the Hindenburg Line on September 29, 1918. Losses of these tanks were heavy and totaled 33 by the end of the war, though some were later recovered. There are conflicting reports regarding the number of Mark Vs shipped back to the United States after the war, varying from 28 to 32.

TANK CORPS DISBANDED

In the aftermath of the Great War, the US Army found itself with a substantial tank force, including over a thousand light tanks and over a hundred heavy tanks. The "war to end all wars" led to considerable controversy in Army planning. The rising wave of isolationism in the country suggested that there would be no future

A cross-sectional view of the Mark VIII heavy tank.

involvement in high-intensity conflict in Europe and that the Army would probably return to its usual role as a frontier constabulary on the Mexican border and in the colonies such as the Philippines. Under such circumstances, the need for a separate Tank Corps was viewed as an unaffordable luxury. From the AEF's limited experiences in 1918, tanks were not regarded as a decisive weapon, and many believed that they were not worth the cost or expense. The National Defense Act of 1920 subordinated the Tank Corps to the Infantry branch. The majority of deployed tanks served in companies attached to the regular Infantry divisions, with another 15 light tank companies scattered around the country with the National Guard. By the mid-1920s, there were less than 500 tanks in service and the rest were in storage. For example, at the end of 1926 there were 320 Six-Ton tanks and 72 Mk VIII heavy tanks in regular Army units plus 110 Six-Ton tanks in the National Guard. The former head of the AEF Tank Corps, Col S. D. Rockenbach, headed the Tank School at Camp Meade with a light and heavy tank battalion. The Infantry School at Fort Benning had a single tank battalion for training purposes.

A comparison of the more common armament variations on the Six-Ton tank M1917: (1) the early 37mm gun mount; (2) the later 37mm gun mount with shield; (3) the early Marlin machine-gun mount; (4) the later Browning machine gun in the 9in ball mount with shield.

In a scene more reminiscent of the Argonne in 1918 than coastal Virginia, a platoon of Six-Ton tanks take part in the Mechanized Force maneuvers at Fort Eustis in the summer of 1931. The tank in the left foreground is one of the Six-Ton tank M1971A1s fitted with the more powerful Franklin engine, as is evident from the added cooling grills on the engine deck. Curiously enough, this exercise was conducted around the trenches built by the British forces under Gen Cornwallis during the final battle of the American Revolution at Yorktown in October 1781.

Under these circumstances, tank development was starved for funds and new tank construction ended for nearly a decade except for prototypes. From the end of the war in 1918 to 1928, the Army spent only $3.5 million on mechanization. Of this, only about $950,000 was spent on tanks and the rest on artillery tractors and artillery self-propelled mounts.

The tanks left over from World War I were far from ideal. Rockenbach viewed the Renault FT and Six-Ton tanks as too small and mechanically unreliable. The Mark VIII Liberty tanks were too slow, too heavy, too long, and too unreliable. The Mark V was widely regarded as the best of the wartime types, but there were too few and they were soon put in storage. Rockenbach wanted a new medium tank that could fulfill the role of both light and heavy tanks. An unstated but widely understood requirement was the need to improve the durability of new tanks. The World War I types were too much like medieval siege engines – useful for a single battle but quickly worn out. The tracks on the heavy tanks had to be replaced after 20 miles of use and the light tanks had to be rebuilt after 80 miles of operation. The early tanks were so mechanically undependable that the Army used tank carriers to move them any appreciable distance to preserve their meager operating life.

The Six-Ton tank M1917 formed the bulk of the tank force and so was the subject of continual upgrade efforts. One of the first upgrade programs was to replace the original Marlin machine gun with the Browning machine gun. Some tanks had adaptations to permit the Browning to be fitted to the existing Marlin mount. Eventually a ball mount with an added armored cover was developed in 1919 that became the standard type. The French offered the Kégresse rubber track upgrade for the light tanks, and one such conversion was undertaken in 1925. Although it did improve the automotive

B

1: MARK V* HEAVY TANK, B COMPANY, 301ST TANK BATTALION AEF, FRANCE, LE CATELET-GOUY, 29 SEPTEMBER 1918

The Mark V tanks used by the 301st Tank Battalion were left in their original British colors and markings. The tanks were painted an overall dark brown. The markings consisted of the white/red/white identification markings on the hull front, repeated on the roofs of the driver's compartment and center commander's cupola. The vehicle serial number was painted in white on either hull side. It was repeated in black on a white rectangle above the machine-gun mounting on the rear plate. This particular tank was commanded by Lt Kusener and it was knocked out by a mine that day before reaching the Hindenburg Line.

2: MARK VIII HEAVY TANK, F COMPANY, 67TH INFANTRY REGIMENT (HEAVY TANKS), FORT BENNING, GEORGIA, 1935

The Mark VIII heavy tanks were finished in overall Specification 3-1 olive drab on their completion at Rock Island Arsenal, the darker postwar shade of the color. Prior to their retirement, the Mark VIII in the 67th Infantry usually had three markings: a white registration number on the hull side, a tactical number on the upper superstructure, and the regimental crest on the sponson.

1

2

performance of the Renault FT, funds were still scarce and priority was given to developing a new light tank. An effort was begun later in the decade to replace the troublesome Buda 40hp engine with a Franklin 67hp engine. A pilot was converted at the Holabird Depot in 1929 and six more tanks were upgraded in 1930–31 as the M1917A1. Other minor upgrades were undertaken on the Six-Ton tank fleet, including various experimental radio mounts.

The durability of early tanks was so poor that the US Army assigned a tank carrier to each tank to move it any long distances. This is a Mack TC-SW of A Company, 1st Tank Regiment carrying a Six-Ton tank M1917 as part of the Mechanized Force at Fort Eustis in August 1931.

EARLY CHRISTIE TANKS

The lack of funds for modern tank development did not deter at least one engineer from offering the US Army his own designs. J. Walter Christie was a colorful and eccentric automobile designer who had built over a dozen self-propelled artillery mounts for Ordnance between 1918 and 1919. Christie's most famous innovation was the "convertible" suspension. Christie came up with the idea for a hybrid suspension that utilized large road-wheels for road travel; on reaching the battlefield, a set of tracks would be mounted for cross-country travel. As a result, the tank carriers would no longer be needed, saving a great deal of money. Christie's Front Drive Motor Company in Hoboken, New Jersey, received a contract for its M1919 convertible tank in November 1919 that was delivered in February 1921 to Aberdeen Proving Ground (APG) in Maryland. The idler and drive sprocket at the ends of the suspension were quite large, while in the center was a bogie with a pair of small road-wheels. The M1919 convertible tank had a simple cylindrical turret with the standard 2.24in M1920 gun, a derivative of the British 6-pdr. The trials in the wheeled configuration were unimpressive since the large road-wheels were rigidly mounted without springs. It was woefully underpowered and barely able to reach 7mph. In April 1921, after two

The Christie M1919 attempted to adapt the convertible chassis developed for previous self-propelled gun mounts as a tank. It was armed with a 2.24in gun in a conventional turret.

months of disappointing tests, Christie asked for the trials to be suspended so that he could improve the design. Ordnance agreed and after nearly a year, the tank was returned to APG for further trials. Now called the M1921 convertible tank, Christie had modified the front road-wheels with substantial springs for a smoother road ride. The hull had been completely reconfigured with the turret replaced with a fixed barbette. The 2.24in gun was mounted in the bow, and two

machine guns were placed in ball mounts in the forward part of the superstructure. Although the alterations did improve the automotive performance, the Army felt that the tank was still underpowered, that its maneuverability was poor, and that the tank was mechanically unreliable.

Ordnance developed a strong distaste for working with Christie. The designer regarded himself as a genius and his designs beyond reproach. He often refused to make changes requested by Ordnance. He did not have the perseverance or patience to convert an intriguing design into a functional and reliable machine. The M1921 convertible tank was retired to the APG museum in July 1924, having cost the US Army some $82,000 not counting test costs. Near bankruptcy, Christie sold off his present and future patent rights for vehicle designs to the Army for $100,000 and reorganized his company as the US Wheel Track Layer Corporation in Rahway, New Jersey. Chief of Ordnance Maj Gen Clarence Williams complained that the Army had paid Christie $839,000, netting the inventor a large profit while the Army did not have a single successful vehicle in service based on a Christie design.

The Christie M1919 tank was completely rebuilt as the M1921 with turret replaced by a barbette mount with a 2.24in gun on the bow and .30cal Browning machine guns on either side. It is being inspected here by Army officers during a demonstration at Camp Meade, with a Mark VIII heavy tank evident in the background.

Christie also worked on a variety of amphibious vehicles, and this is his second design, the Combined Wheel and Self-propelled Floating Type 75mm Gun Motor Carriage Model 1922. Christie is seen here on the left speaking to Secretary of the Navy Edwin Denby in the hopes of winning a contract from the Marine Corps.

ROCK ISLAND ARSENAL TANKS

The Army's first postwar tank design was the M1921 medium tank, also sometimes called Tank A. It was armed with a 2.24in gun in the turret with a .30cal Browning machine gun in the cupola above.

The Army's tank development in the interwar years was centered at Rock Island Arsenal (RIA) in Illinois. Rockenbach favored the development of a new medium tank, and the program began in 1919. The head of the RIA design section at the time was Maj Levin Campbell, who would lead Ordnance in World War II. The new design was heavily influenced by the British Medium D tank. The pilot medium tank M1921 was completed at RIA in December 1921 and delivered to APG for trials. It weighed about 22 tons, and its main armament was the 2.24in M1920 gun. The Murray & Tregurtha 220hp engine proved to be underpowered and unreliable. The second pilot, the medium tank M1922, entered trials at APG in March 1923. It introduced a novel flexible cable track inspired by a British design. These pilots were used as test-beds over the next several years. Lessons from these tanks led to the construction of the T1 medium tank, which introduced a new 200hp Packard tank engine specially commissioned for tank use. This tank closely resembled the M1921 and was completed in May 1927. The new engine offered such improvement in performance that the Ordnance Committee recommended standardization as the M1 medium tank, which took place in February 1928. This standardization decision was withdrawn later in 1928 in no small measure due to resistance from the Corps of Engineers, who complained that the tank was too heavy for tactical bridging. Rockenbach had already left his influential tank school post, and support for a medium tank had weakened in favor of a smaller and cheaper light tank.

C

1: T1E1 MEDIUM TANK, F COMPANY, 67TH INFANTRY REGIMENT (HEAVY TANKS), FORT BENNING, GEORGIA, 1934

This tank was painted in the standard postwar olive drab. The March 1922 Infantry (Tanks) insignia was rescinded on August 22, 1933 and replaced with a simplified design using the plain Infantry crossed-rifles insignia with the company letter above and the regiment number below. The 67th Infantry also began the practice of naming their tanks starting with the company letter, in this case "Fu Manchu" based on the character from the popular adventure novels. Many tanks at Fort Benning in the mid-1930s were painted with the vehicle designation, presumably as a means of educating troops about the new tanks.

2: T1E1 LIGHT TANK, F COMPANY, 2ND TANK REGIMENT (HEAVY TANKS), FORT BENNING, GEORGIA, 1932

Although originally equipped with Mark VIII heavy tanks, in the early 1930s this unit served as a trials unit for the assorted new tank types including the T1 light tank series. In March 1922, the Adjutant General had approved a new design for Infantry (tanks) consisting of "the Infantry insignia (crossed rifles) with tank superimposed." This is the marking seen here, with the battalion number above and company letter below. As in the case of other new types at Fort Benning, the tank designation was painted on the tank, in this case on the bow.

1

MEDIUM - T1E1

67
F

FU-MANCHU

2

2
F

T1E1

67
F

2
F

LEFT
The T1 medium tank closely resembled the M1921, but the use of the more powerful Packard engine required changes in the engine deck configuration, as seen here during field trials at RIA in June 1927.

RIGHT
Four T1E1 light tanks served with A Company, 1st Tank Regiment, attached to the Mechanized Force at Fort Eustis in the summer of 1931.

In September 1923, the Ordnance Department hired an automobile designer, Harry A. Knox, to head its automotive development at RIA. Knox was 48 years old at the time and had been the founder of the Knox Automobile Company in Springfield, Massachusetts, which manufactured a wide range of automobiles and trucks prior to World War I. Knox would go on to become the most important American tank designer of the pre-World War II period, and was responsible for most of the essential features of American tank designs such as the vertical volute suspension, rubber block track and a host of other designs.

Knox's first major project was the T1 light tank. It was intended to provide significantly greater durability than the Six-Ton tank M1917 and the armament was upgraded to include both a 37mm gun and a coaxial machine gun in a combination mount. The chassis was also intended to serve as the basis for a family of vehicles, including a cargo tractor, mortar carrier, and possibly self-propelled artillery. The most noticeable differences from the previous light tanks was the decision to use a front-mounted engine. Trials of the T1 in 1927 and 1928 were successful enough that a test batch of six more vehicles was authorized, consisting of four T1E1 light tanks and two T1E1 cargo carriers. Due to the complexity of the design, the manufacturing of these tanks was put

The T2 medium tank resembled an enlarged version of the T1E1 light tank. It carried a 47mm gun in the turret and a 37mm gun in the hull. Among its more unusual features was the location of the fuel tanks on the exterior of the hull above the suspension.

out to bid to the major automobile companies. None wanted to be bothered with such a puny order. James Cunningham, of Son and Company in Rochester, New York, was the sole bidder and winner of the contract. The four T1E1 light tanks were deployed at Fort Meade, and to prove their durability, they conducted a road march to Gettysburg, averaging 10 miles per hour on the 145-mile course. One of the tanks on trials at APG completed over 2,000 miles of tests over two months without serious breakdown. This was an astounding improvement over the Six-Ton tanks, which on average had to be rebuilt every 80 miles. The successful trials on the tanks led to their standardization as the M1 light tank in January 1928, but, as in the case of the M1 medium tank, standardization was withdrawn shortly afterwards due to several factors described below.

The T1E1 was succeeded by the T1E2 in 1929. This increased the armor from ⅜ to ⅝in, increased horsepower from 110 to 132hp, and improved the suspension and other features. Infantry tactics at the time favored tanks firing on the move. The existing short 37mm M1916 gun in the T1 combination mount was not likely to hit its targets and had a slow rate of fire. This led to some interest in a semi-automatic gun, and the T1E2 introduced the Browning 37mm E2 Auto-Gun M1924 that fired from a five-round clip. Infantry complaints about the rough cross-country performance of these tanks led to the design of a spring-hydraulic suspension that was fitted to the T1E3 in 1931.

Comparative Technical Data – US Tanks of the 1920s				
	Six-Ton M1917	Christie M1921	T1 medium	T1E1 light
Crew	2	2	4	2
Length	16ft 5in	18ft 2in	21ft 6in	12ft 8in
Width	5ft 9in	8ft 4in	8ft	5ft 10in
Height	7ft 7in	6ft 10in	9ft 8in	7ft 2in
Weight (tons)	7.2	12.6	21.9	7.8
Engine (hp)	42	120	200	110
Max speed (mph)	5	13	14	17
Main gun	37mm M1916 or MG	2.24in M1920	2.24in M1920	37mm M1916
Machine guns	0	1	1	1
Max. armor (mm)	15	12	25	10

THE CHRISTIE DISTRACTION

Corps of Engineer concerns over the weight of the T1 medium tank led to the start of the new 15-ton T2 medium tank in 1926. Lack of funding delayed construction until 1929. Designed by Harry Knox and built by Cunningham, it resembled an enlarged T1E2 light tank. It had thicker armor and was armed with a 3-pdr (47mm) naval gun. It also had a 37mm gun in the right hull front, but this was quickly replaced with a .30cal machine gun since the gun mount interfered with the turret crew. With a 312hp Liberty aircraft engine, it had a very peppy performance with road speeds up to 25mph. Nevertheless, the T2 quickly disappeared due to Infantry distaste over front-mounted engine designs, engineer complaints about its weight, and the appearance of the rival Christie tank.

After the failure of his M1919 and M1921 tanks, Christie spent several years trying to perfect his convertible suspension. The new design, patented in April 1928, used identical large road-wheels on all stations except the idler and drive sprocket. When the track was removed, the last road-wheel station was powered by a chain-drive off the drive sprocket while the front road-wheel steered the vehicle. The suspension used large helical springs, mounted in protected tunnels within the armored hull, which provided a particularly smooth ride compared to the suspensions that predominated in tank design at this time. To address the Army's criticism of the sluggish performance of the M1921, Christie used a surplus 300hp Liberty aircraft engine, which he claimed would permit a road speed of 70mph on wheels and 42mph on tracks. The M1928 was not a refined tank, having a bow-mounted machine gun that interfered with the driver. In addition, its flashy performance was due in part to its light weight of about 5 tons made possible by the use of thin sheet steel instead of armor. Christie dubbed the new tank variously the M1928 and M1940, the later designation chosen to show that it was a decade more advanced than any contemporary tank design.

Christie's M1928 tank was first displayed to the public on July 4, 1928. It appeared at a fortuitous moment when there was a groundswell from younger Army tank enthusiasts beginning to challenge the lethargy and doctrinal orthodoxy of the past decade. In 1927, Secretary of War Dwight Davis witnessed Britain's Experimental Mechanized Force at Aldershot during an official visit to the UK. On his return, he instructed the US Army to conduct a similar exercise, and this began in the summer of 1928 at Camp Meade. The new T1E1 light tanks proved to be reliable performers compared to the decrepit WWI-era tanks. Nevertheless, many younger officers were concerned that they offered little advance over the Six-Ton tank. In contrast, the performance of Christie's "wildcat" tank seemed miraculous and offered the technological promise of an escape from the horrors of static trench warfare and a new dawn of mobile offensive warfare.

Like many entrepreneurs, Christie was fond of publicity stunts. To show his tank's superiority over the Army's T1E1 light tank, he made the same trip from Fort Meade, Maryland, to Gettysburg, Pennsylvania, in November 1928 with an average speed of 28 miles per hour compared to 10mph for the Ordnance tank. Patton and some of the young Cavalry firebrands recommended that the Christie vehicle be acquired as an armored car, suggesting that it would be particularly useful in patrolling the border with

Mexico. On February 19, 1929, Secretary of War Davis directed Ordnance to purchase the M1928 in an armored car configuration and modest funds were approved in the Fiscal Year 1929 (FY29) budget.[1] Disdainful of the Ordnance bureaucracy, Christie provided the M1928 at no cost to the Tank School at Fort Meade for testing but ignored Ordnance's May 1929 request for bids. As a result, the allotted funds reverted to the Treasury, delaying any purchase for at least another year until funding could be re-approved by Congress. Christie belatedly responded in July 1929 that he had spent $382,000 on the project and so he wanted to sell eight of the tanks at a cost of $82,750 each, which amounted to a development cost of $47,750 each plus the actual manufacturing cost of $35,000 per tank. This was an impossible sum at the time, particularly after the advent of the Great Depression late in 1929.

Christie received a contract for a single M1930 tank that was subjected to trials by the US Army in 1931 prior to a production contract. Christie retained ownership of this particular tank and he later sold it to Morris Motors in Britain, where it served as the basis for the A13 and subsequent cruiser tanks.

Christie had been soliciting bids from foreign governments at the same time as his promotions to the US government. A Polish purchasing mission was offered one tank for $30,000 plus a further $90,000 for manufacturing rights, and Warsaw submitted a down payment. The Soviet Union was also bidding for the tank and on April 28, 1930 purchased two M1930 tanks at a cost of $30,000 each, plus $100,000 for manufacturing rights.

Changes in Army leadership roiled the negotiations. The new Army Chief of Infantry, General Stephen Fuqua, was very supportive of acquiring the Christie tanks and as a result, the Ordnance Technical Committee on February 13, 1930 recommended the purchase of six M1928s in a tank configuration with turret. The $250,000 in the FY31 budget earmarked for the purchase of six to eight Cunningham T1E2 tanks was redirected to the Christie tanks instead. The incoming Chief of Ordnance, Gen Samuel Hof, was an old Ordnance hand who had been involved in the squabbles with Christie in the early 1920s. Based on a critical report from tank expert Capt John Christmas, Hof was skeptical of the durability of the Christie tank and wanted to acquire only a single tank for trials before buying any more. In June 1930, the Army Chief of Staff, Gen Charles Summerall, agreed with Hof. Christie was informed that his May 1930 bid for six convertible tanks and a new armored car had been rejected. Instead, he was asked to make an offer for a single tank. Christie responded that he would sell a single tank for the exorbitant price of $135,000, and further angered the Army officers involved in the negotiations by claiming that he had "spies" in the Army and government who kept him informed of the inner workings of the negotiations. He also threatened to use his political connections in Congress to pressure the Army into agreeing to a large purchase.

With the end of the fiscal year approaching and the FY31 tank funding about to revert back to the Treasury again, Christie acquiesced to a lease deal. Contract Word 89, valued at $55,000, was signed on June 28, 1930

1   The federal Fiscal Year ran from July 1 to June 30, so FY29 was July 1, 1928, to June 30, 1929.

A pair of T3E1 convertible tanks in the road-travel mode with their tracks stowed. They belonged to F Company, 67th Infantry Regiment (Heavy Tanks), and were seen here during the First Army maneuvers at Pine Camp, New York, in August 1935. Tank No. 2 Tornado is in front and Tank No. 6 Hurricane behind it.

with Christie promising to deliver a single convertible tank for trials purposes while the Army would provide the Liberty engine and a suitable turret. The contract mandated a September 1930 delivery date.

Christie was unable to make the deadline since he was already behind schedule on the delivery of the two Soviet tanks; he reneged on the Polish contract in October 1930. He dispatched the two Soviet "commercial tractors" on December 24, 1930. The Army learned of Christie's duplicity as well as the much lower price he was offering to foreign buyers, further souring relations. The American M1930 Christie tank was delivered behind schedule to APG on January 19, 1931. The Liberty engine broke down after two days of testing, further delaying the trials. The powertrain was a constant source of problems on the Christie design since the engine was too powerful for the transmission; the Soviets had the same problem.[2]

Egged on by Christie and his many supporters in the Army, Representative Henry Barbour, the chairman of the House sub-committee on appropriations, held extensive Congressional hearings on the Christie tank in December 1930. Col Hiram Cooper, commandant of the Infantry Tank School, strongly praised the Christie tank, as did Sereno Brett, a decorated World War I tanker and executive officer of the Experimental Mechanized Force at Fort Meade. Capt Llewellyn Tharp, who had commanded a company of American Mark V tanks in France in 1918, gave extensive testimony why the Christie tank was so much superior to Ordnance's T1E1, which he had also tested.

2   For an account of the Soviet experience with the Christie tank, see Steven J. Zaloga, *New Vanguard 237: BT Fast Tank: The Red Army's Cavalry Tank 1931–45* (Osprey, 2016).

When Christie refused to upgrade the T3 convertible tank to Infantry specifications, American LaFrance was given the contract to build the T3E2 convertible tank. As can be seen, one of the main changes was to widen the hull to accommodate a four-man crew.

Congressional pressure as well as support for the Christie tank from the Infantry and Cavalry branches forced Ordnance to purchase a larger batch of Christie tanks. Competitive bids were opened on June 4, 1931 and submissions were received from Christie and Nicholas Straussler from Britain. With Barbour's political support, it was a foregone conclusion that Christie would win the bid. On June 12, 1931 Christie was informed that his firm had won the negotiations and would receive $241,500 in FY32 for seven convertible tanks.

Testing of the new serial production tanks began in December 1931. Of the seven Christie tanks in Army hands, three were designated as T3 medium tanks and allotted to the Infantry at Fort Benning. The remaining four were designated as T1 Combat Cars and sent to the Cavalry at Fort Knox. The first tank used a chain-drive to power the rear wheel when in road travel, but Christie switched to a gear drive on the remaining six tanks, leading to a change of designation to the T3E1 medium tank. The tanks were hand-crafted and different problems cropped up on different tanks. Christie spent far more time on "lawyering and lobbying" and not enough time on quality control at his plant. Furthermore, he resisted Ordnance efforts to make improvements on designs which he regarded as unquestionably flawless.

The Infantry wanted at least five tanks to create a normal tank platoon for field experiments. They also wanted a number of significant improvements, including a wider hull to accommodate a four-man crew. As a result, in October 1932, the Army issued a contract bid for five more tanks designated as T3E2. Christie was unwilling to make such extensive changes, and became infuriated when Ordnance sent the bid requests to more than a dozen companies. He believed that he still controlled the patent rights, ignoring previous Army payments. Ordnance anticipated legal action and had already been assured by government lawyers that a tank derived from the Christie concepts was within the Army's legal rights. Christie refused to participate in the bidding and American LaFrance in Elmira, New York, won the contract on December 2, 1932 for $146,000 for five T3E2 tanks.

Christie began a political campaign to get the contract annulled, which dragged on for several years. He had alienated Gen Hof, and many of Christie's supporters in the Army came to realize that the convertible tanks were poorly made. They quickly became "hangar queens," requiring constant maintenance. The diary of Robert Grow, later commander of the 6th Armored Division, recalled the problems with the new tanks: "Had three Christies running this AM. Took them out for rehearsal. Two promptly broke down. No. 3 Christie

The last of the convertible tanks was the T4, seen here without its armament. It was belatedly standardized as the M1 medium tank, but few were built due to its high cost and skepticism about the value of the convertible feature.

Three of the T4 convertible tanks were constructed in the T4E1 barbette configuration, later serving with F Company, 67th Infantry Regiment (Medium Tank) at Fort Benning. This is the pilot; the final configuration used a common road-wheel like that on the first and last station. This particular vehicle is armed with one of the early Browning T2 .50cal machine guns with barrel-cooling fins.

Technical Data

Crew	2: driver, gunner/commander
Length	18ft
Width	7ft 4in
Height	7ft 6in
Main gun	37mm Model 1916 in T1 combination mount
Elevation	15-degree elevation and depression; 15-degree traverse
Secondary armament	coaxial .30cal Browning machine gun
Ammunition	126 rounds 37mm, 3,000 rounds .30cal
Armor	⅝in vertical surfaces, ½in horizontal and sloping surfaces
Fuel	89 gallons
Engine	Liberty 12-cyl. V-type, 338hp at 1,400rpm
Speed (wheels)	46.7mph
Speed (tracks)	27.2mph
Ground pressure	8.33psi

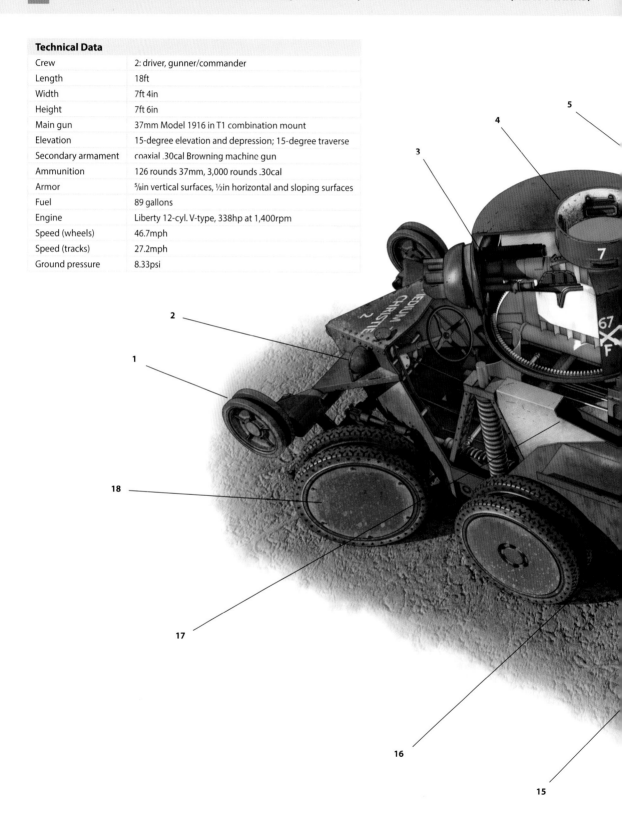

1. Front idler wheel
2. Front headlight
3. 37mm Model 1916 in T1 combination mount with co-axial .30 cal Browning machine gun
4. Commander's vision cupola
5. Radio aerial

6. Liberty 12 cyl. V-type engine
7. Cover for radiator fill cap
8. Armored cover over radiator opening
9. Armored flaps over air intake
10. Tracks in stowed, road-travel mode
11. Muffler
12. Transmission

13. Rear drive sprocket
14. Engine cooling fan
15. Cavity for suspension spring
16. Left fuel tank
17. Radiator
18. Steerable front road-wheel

The last attempt to redeem the Christie suspension was the T7 project in 1938. This mounted a new suspension with pneumatic tires to a M1A1 Combat Car. It was rejected by the Cavalry because by this stage the durability of the basic M1A1 precluded the need for such expensive approaches.

broke a crankshaft and camrod and tore the crankshaft open. A mean job. 19th Ordnance is pulling the engine." Ordnance publicized the fact that the Army had to spend more than $38,000 to rectify problems on the Christie tanks in 1932 due to inherent defects.

In the end, the US Army refused to have any further dealings with Christie, and his company went into receivership in 1934. Christie was saved from bankruptcy by a request from Morris Motors in October 1936. British military attachés in the Soviet Union had seen a display of the BT-5 tanks in 1936 and there was Army interest in a British Christie tank. Christie still officially owned the Contract Word 89 tank and delivered this to the UK as a "farm tractor" plus manufacturing rights for $320,000. This led to the A-13 and a subsequent line of Cruiser tanks such as the Covenanter, Crusader, Centaur, and Cromwell.

The American LaFrance T3E2 bore a family resemblance to the Christie design except that the hull had been widened to accept a four-man crew. In many ways, this paralleled the Soviet experience with the BT series that had evolved into the A-20, later leading to the T-34 tank of World War II. The Liberty engine used on the Christie tanks was replaced by a 435hp Curtiss D-12 aircraft engine that provided a maximum speed of 58mph on wheels and 35mph on track. New forged link tracks with a shorter pitch were used that reduced the tendency of the tank to shed its track compared to the archaic plate tracks of the Christie tank. The T3E2 suffered the same inherent problem of the Christie design, mating too powerful an engine with too delicate a transmission and final drive. Clutch-and-brake steering was inadequate for such a powerful powertrain. All five tanks had improvements and were designated as the T3E3 afterwards.

The next attempt to redeem the Christie design was the T4 convertible tank, designed by Knox's team at RIA. To get around the powertrain problems, a less powerful 268hp Continental engine was used, with a new transmission with controlled differential steering. These tanks proved to be the most successful of the Christie-inspired tanks and also the most numerous, with 19 produced at RIA in 1936 and 1937. Three of these were built in the T4E1 configuration, which used a barbette configuration instead of a turret. Ordnance recommended standardizing these tanks in February 1936, but this was rejected on the grounds that they were not better armed or armored than the M2 light tank, but cost twice as much. This issue was raised again in 1939 and as a result they were designated as the M1 medium tank. This design might have evolved into a modern medium tank as occurred in the Soviet Union with the T-34. However, the Infantry branch was complacent about the need for greater firepower and improved armor due to its antiquated tank doctrine. The Cavalry wanted the T4, but were unable to buy any due to budget constraints.

After testing the Vickers Six-Ton tank in 1931, the T1 light tank was completely reconfigured as the T1E4, seen here at RIA in March 1932.

KNOX'S LIGHT TANKS

Knox's T1E1 light tank of 1928 represented a major step forward in durability over existing tank types, but the program suffered a series of setbacks in 1928–29. After a short-lived decision to standardize the type as the M1 light tank, the decision was rescinded due in part to Infantry criticism of its unorthodox front-mounted engine. Infantry officers were not happy about the driver sitting so far back in the hull and there were complaints about exhaust fumes leaking into the fighting compartment and fouling the gun's sights. The archaic suspension offered a very rough cross-country ride. Ordnance plans to procure six to eight T1E1 tanks with FY30 funding fell through when the money was diverted to the Christie project. The Soviet Union was on the verge of signing a contract with the Cunningham company in February 1930 to purchase 50 of the improved T1E2 tanks, but this deal was abandoned after the Soviet purchasing commission witnessed a demonstration of the impressive Christie tank in April 1930.

In June 1931, Ordnance tested Britain's new Vickers Six-Ton tank Type A at APG. This was one of the most modern tanks of the time, and its semi-elliptic leaf spring suspension and narrow-pitch track offered a much superior ride to the existing Ordnance designs. There was some concern over the fragility of the suspension so Knox designed a new spring suspension patterned on the Vickers design, receiving a patent in March 1933. To address the Infantry concerns over the T1E2 layout, Knox completely redesigned the next iteration, the T1E4, with a more conventional rear-mounted engine. Tests revealed it to be underpowered, in part due to power loss when using the conventional clutch-and-brake steering system. This was addressed by mounting

The M2A1 light tank was short-lived after the Infantry decided they preferred twin-turreted tanks. It had a smaller turret like that of the parallel Cavalry combat cars.

a more powerful LaFrance 244hp engine in its successor, the T1E6. A Cleveland Tractor controlled-differential transmission was demonstrated in the T1E5 test-bed and led to the recommendation that this approach be taken in all future American tank designs. Although the T1 series had been instrumental in creating an effective tank design team at RIA, no serial production took place. The T1E6 weighed 10 tons, and in the spring of 1933, the Secretary of War, under Engineer pressure, instructed Ordnance to limit future tanks and combat cars to 7.5 tons.

The M1 Combat Car resembled the Infantry's light tanks, but used a larger turret with the two machine guns on separate mounts. The original production series used curved plates. This is a combat car of the 1st Cavalry Regiment (Mecz) at Fort Knox in 1936.

COMBAT CARS AND INFANTRY TANKS

The Mechanized Force at Fort Eustis concluded its maneuvers in the summer of 1931. Douglas MacArthur, the new Army chief of staff, rejected pleas by some of the Cavalry visionaries such as Adna Chaffee for a permanent Mechanized Force, and it was disbanded in October 1931. Instead, MacArthur approved plans by both the Cavalry and Infantry to undertake mechanization on their own paths. Since the Cavalry was not allowed tanks under the 1920 Congressional edict, this obstacle was avoided by designating the Cavalry tanks as "combat cars." Due to a shortage of funds, both the Infantry and Cavalry were obliged to rely on a common RIA light tank design, differing mainly in the turret design.

The end of the T1 light tank program and the MacArthur mechanization decision started a new light tank program in June 1933 that would result in the most enduring and successful American light tanks of the interwar years. This program was slow in emerging due to funding cuts stemming from the Great Depression. But it would establish many of the signature technologies of American tanks of World War II, mostly designed by Harry Knox. There

1: M1 COMBAT CAR, HQ, C TROOP, 1ST CAVALRY REGIMENT, FORT KNOX, 1936
The two Cavalry regiments of the 7th Cavalry Brigade were distinguished by their regimental insignia. The commander's vehicle usually carried the Cavalry guidon, painted on a sheet metal plate and attached to the front of the turret. This included the regimental number above and the troop letter below. The 1st Cavalry also used a set of tactical symbols for the platoons, painted in yellow on the turret front and again on the rear turret corner. This included a circle (HQ); I (1st Platoon); inverted T (2nd Platoon); triangle (3rd Platoon); and square (4th Platoon). This shows the old pattern AR 850-5-style of markings with the unit identity printed on the turret between two white bars. This combat car lacks the usual registration numbers.

2: M1A1 COMBAT CAR, E TROOP, 13TH CAVALRY REGIMENT, FORT KNOX, 1938
The later style of unit marking, as seen here, was the troop letter painted on the turret front in a large size. This is the E Troop commander's combat car, and so has the usual guidon fixed to the turret front. Combat car registration numbers were in the sequence 40xxx. As in the case of the Infantry tanks, Cavalry combat cars had the Cavalry crossed-sabers attached as a small brass plaque.

1

2

The M1A1 Combat Car was essentially similar to the M1, but the turret was constructed of flat armor plates. This vehicle served with C Troop, 1st Cavalry Regiment (Mecz) during the Third Army maneuvers in 1940. The large "2" painted on the bow was for aerial recognition during the wargame.

were two pilots for this series, both sharing common powertrains and similar hull designs. The powerplant was a Continental radial aircraft engine and the steering used a controlled-differential. The Infantry's T2 light tank used Knox's spring suspension inspired by the Vickers design, while the Cavalry's T5 Combat Car used a new Knox invention, a vertical volute suspension. While the pilots first used a conventional steel track, Knox designed a novel rubber block track with rubber bushings, later standardized as the T16 track. These features would become characteristic of American light and medium tanks for nearly a decade. In the event, the trials favored the more robust Knox vertical volute suspension over the Vickers-style suspension and the T2 light tank was suitably altered as the T2E1.

This family of light tanks and combat cars also marked a shift away from the old 37mm M1916 gun to the new Browning .50cal heavy machine gun as their principal armament. The old French 37mm gun had never been intended for tank fighting and its armor-piercing round was barely capable of penetrating 15mm (⅝in) armor even at 100 yards. The air-cooled T2 machine gun had been developed at Springfield Armory for the Cavalry as their principal antitank weapon both for horse transport and vehicle applications. Its projectile had been based on the German World War I 13mm antitank rifle projectile and the armor-piercing round could penetrate 28mm (1.1in) of armor at 100 yards and 25mm (1in) at 500 yards. Ordnance recommended it for standardization in November 1933 as the .50cal M2 HB (heavy barrel). Aside from its superior armor penetration compared to the old 37mm gun, its high rate of fire was a substantial advantage. US tank doctrine in the 1930s recommended fire-on-the-move tactics; a machine gun compensated for the inevitable inaccuracy inherent in such a tactic compared to a single-shot, slow-firing gun. The .50cal was subsequently accepted by the Infantry for the same role. After further improvements, both the T2E1 and T5 were accepted for serial production as the M2A1 light tank and M1 Combat Car. A total of nine M2A1 light tanks and 33 M1 Combat Cars were manufactured at RIA from the FY36 budget.

CAVALRY COMBAT CARS

The M1 Combat Cars were deployed with the 1st Cavalry (Mecz) and saw their first real display during the Second Army summer maneuvers in 1936. After initial maneuvers at Fort Knox, the 1st Cavalry (Mecz) made a 375-mile road march to Camp Custer, Michigan, a testament to the durability of the new generation of tanks. The Cavalry also wanted to begin purchasing the T4 convertible tank, but due to its cost, this plan was abandoned. A new convertible tank, the T6, was designed, but its weight and twin-turret configuration led to its cancelation in November 1935 before a pilot was built. In its place, RIA began to adapt the existing M1 Combat Car by switching to the convertible configuration as the T7 Combat Car. Unlike previous convertible tanks which had employed solid rubber rims on their metal wheels, the T7 used a novel type of pneumatic tire to provide a smoother ride. This was designed by Capt John Christmas, later to be instrumental in the design of the M4 Sherman tank. The pilot of the T7 arrived at APG for trials in August 1938, and a year later, it took part in the First Army wargames near Plattsburgh, New York. By this time, the existing combat cars had proven durable enough for long road marches and the Mechanized Cavalry Board recommended a termination of efforts on convertible tanks due to their high cost and complexity.

Technical evolution of the M1 Combat Car continued, mainly aimed at cutting costs and improving service life. Ordnance had been studying the use of the 250hp Guiberson T-1020 radial diesel engine, since it promised greater engine life and lower cost. Three combat cars were built as the M1E1 with diesel engines in FY37 and a further seven in FY38. The most visible change in the combat cars was the decision to shift from a cylindrical turret to a polygonal turret. This was primarily due to the cost and complexity of dealing with curved armor steel, and the same process was undertaken with the Infantry's light tanks. The combat cars with this feature were designated as M1A1 and they were manufactured in FY38.

To further reduce the ground pressure of the combat cars, Harry Knox had developed a trailing idler wheel design. Another improvement was the

A local resident of Manchester, Tennessee, looks on with curiosity at a tank taking part in the Second Army maneuvers there in June 1941. This vehicle was originally designated as the M2 Combat Car, but was redesignated as the M1A1 light tank after the absorption of the Cavalry tanks into the Armored Force the previous summer. This particular tank was the command vehicle of Maj Gen George S. Patton, commander of the 2nd Armored Division at this time.

The Infantry switched to twin-turret light tanks in 1935, nicknamed the "Mae West" tank after the popular actress. This M2A2 Model 1936 shows the early cylindrical turrets, as well as the brush guard added to the hull side to shield the tools. This particular tank originally served with the 43rd Tank Company (NG) and became part of the new 191st Tank Battalion at Fort Meade during the September 1940 consolidation. It is seen here on parade in Baltimore, Maryland, in June 1941.

The M2A2 Model 1937 introduced a new turret design using flat plates instead of the curved plates on previous versions. By this stage, the brush guard over the tools on the sponson side was standard. This is a tank from the 1st Armored Division during maneuvers at Fort Knox in 1941.

increase in the turret height to better accommodate the turret crew, called the Improved Cavalry Turret. These new features were incorporated in the FY40 production run as the M2 Combat Car, and 34 were built.

With war clouds brewing in Europe, the Cavalry proposed expanding the 7th Cavalry Brigade (Mecz) into a full mechanized division. To equip this force, the Cavalry recommended the procurement of 292 new combat cars with the Improved Cavalry Turret, protectoscope vision ports as developed for the Infantry tanks, Guiberson diesel engines, and new pistol ports. This version was designated as the M2A1 Combat Car. As an offshoot of this project, the Cavalry proposed upgrading 88 older M1 Combat Cars with the Improved Cavalry Turret as the M1A2 Combat Car. In the event, the Armored Force was created before these plans were realized, and neither the M2A1 nor M1A2 reached the production stage. With the disappearance of the "combat car" designation, the M2 became the M1A1 light tank and the M1 became the M1A2 light tank. The two mechanized Cavalry regiments became the core of the new 1st Armored Division.

INFANTRY LIGHT TANKS

The M2A1 light tank was not popular in Infantry service due to the cramped turret. In the meantime, Ordnance had tested a barbette configuration on one of the T4 pilots as the T4E1, and also a twin-turret design on a T5 pilot as the T2E2. The twin turret was another inspiration from the Vickers Six-Ton "trench sweeper" tank. In the event, the Infantry preferred the twin-turret option and this became the most common configuration for the next several years. The twin-turret configuration was standardized as the M2A2 light tank, with the first ten funded in FY36. This initial production batch was sometimes called the M2A2 Model 1935 since production started in 1935. The next production batch of 124 tanks was unofficially called the M2A2 Model 1936 and was produced mainly in FY37. The final production batch of 104 tanks was called M2A2 Model 1937 and they were funded mainly from the FY38 budget. As mentioned earlier, Ordnance decided to shift from curved plate turret construction to the use of flat armor plate, and this occurred in the M2A2 Model 1937 production run. Early service use of the M2A2 discovered that the tools stowed on the hull sides were knocked off when moving through foliage. As a result, a brush guard was developed to prevent this. This appears as a standard item on the M2A2 Model 1937, though there are examples of a few earlier production tanks with this feature. The M2A2 was the most widely produced version of the twin-turreted Infantry light tanks, totaling 235.

A variety of changes were introduced into the final batch of 73 FY38 Infantry tanks, designated as M2A3. To improve floatation, the bogies were spaced further apart and the rear idler wheel was moved further to the rear.

Modern tanks were in such short supply in the years leading up to World War II that ordinary trucks were sometimes used as substitutes, carrying a large banner on their side. This is the First Army wargame near Winthrop, New York, on August 9, 1940 with a M2A2 Model 1936 light tank of the tank company of the 26th Yankee Division (NG) in the foreground.

Turret armor was thickened from a maximum of ⅝ to ⅞in. The turrets were moved slightly outboard for greater clearance. The engine rear deck was redesigned for better access. Eight of the M2A3 production tanks were powered by Guiberson diesels, designated as M2A3E1.

Comparative Technical Data US – Tanks of the 1930s

	T3 Christie	M2A2 light tank	M1 Combat Car	M1 medium tank	M2A4 light tank	M2A1 medium tank
Crew	2	4	4	4	4	5
Length	18ft	13ft 7in	13ft 7in	16ft 1in	14ft 7in	17ft 8in
Width	7ft 4in	7ft 10in	7ft 10in	8ft 2in	8ft 4in	8ft 7in
Height	7ft 6in	7ft 9in	7ft 5in	7ft 3in	8ft 2in	9ft
Weight (tons)	11.2	9.5	9.4	13.5	12	42
Engine (hp)	338	250	250	268	250	400
Max speed (mph)	47	45	45	35	34	30
Main gun	37mm M1916	.50cal M2HB	.50cal M2HB	.50cal M2HB	37mm M5	37mm M5
Machine guns	1	2	2	2	4	7
Max. armor (mm)	16	16	16	16	25	38

INCREASING ARMOR AND FIREPOWER

The standard US Army antitank weapon up through 1940 was the .50cal M2 heavy machine gun. This was adequate for most tank fighting since 15–20mm tank armor was still widespread in the mid-1930s and the .50cal could penetrate this at normal combat ranges. The Spanish Civil War of 1936–38 saw the first large-scale tank-versus-tank fighting in history. The tanks that took part in this conflict, such as the Soviet T-26 and German

PzKpfw I, were lightly armored. However, the dominant technical lesson from the fighting was that contemporary tanks were too thinly armored to face contemporary antitank guns such as the German 37mm gun or Soviet 45mm guns, and so European armies began building tanks that were resistant to 37mm guns. In 1938, American studies of the lessons of the Spanish conflict concluded that future US tanks should be armed at least with a 37mm gun, and that the armor basis of the vehicle had to be increased from the existing level of ⅝in (16mm) since this could be easily penetrated by a 37mm gun from any realistic combat range. The Infantry had already selected a new 37mm antitank gun and so this was selected as the armament for a new version of the M2 light tank series.[3]

The M2A3 had a significantly redesigned engine deck to provide better access. To lower ground pressure, the track footprint was increased by moving the rear bogie and idler wheel back further.

In December 1938, the Infantry branch authorized the construction of the improved M2A4 light tank, fitted with a single large turret with a 37mm gun, and protected with thicker 1in (25mm) armor. The modestly improved armor was not adequate to protect the tank against 37mm guns, but incorporation of gun-proof armor would have required a complete redesign of the tank, which the Army could not afford. Other important improvements included the incorporation of radio receivers in all tanks, radio transmitters

3   Steven J. Zaloga, New Vanguard 107: *US Anti-tank Artillery 1941–45* (Osprey, 2005).

1: M2A2 LIGHT TANK, 29TH TANK COMPANY, 29TH DIVISION (NG), FIRST ARMY MANEUVERS, AUGUST 1939

National Guard divisional tank companies usually had their identification painted on the front turret sides pursuant to Army Regulation AR 850-5. This was often accompanied by the divisional insignia in color, in this case the "Blue & the Grey" of the 29th Division, symbolizing its roots in the Maryland-Virginia areas that had fought on opposing sides in the American Civil War. The vehicle tactical number was sometimes painted on the tank as well. By the late 1930s, Ordnance had adopted a standardized form of registration numbers to monitor maintenance records, preceded by U.S.A. W (War Department). In the case of the Infantry, the registration number began as 30xxx. The M2A2 series started at 30110 and the M2A2 Model 1937 with the angular, flat-plate turret, as seen here, started around 30265. Unlike later practices where numbers were assigned in contract, the RIA issued the numbers sequentially during production, so medium tank numbers were mixed in with light tanks. The new M2A3 light tank registration numbers began at 30370 and ran to 30442. In November 1937, Ordnance recommended that the new R1XS58A olive drab gloss enamel be adopted as substitute standard for peacetime, while the normal lusterless formulation be retained for wartime use. This olive drab appeared darker to the human eye than the lusterless olive drab even though they both shared the same Specification 3-1 color.

2: M1 MEDIUM TANK, 3RD PLATOON, F COMPANY, 67TH INFANTRY REGIMENT (MEDIUM TANK), THIRD ARMY MANEUVERS, 1940

The 67th Infantry Regiment (Medium Tank) adopted more elaborate markings in the late 1930s. For most of the interwar years, only F Company, 2nd Battalion was active. The company identified the platoons by shape, 1st Platoon (diamond); 2nd Platoon (circle); 3rd Platoon (square). These were marked in yellow with a red border on the hull sides and hull rear with the company letter and again with the vehicle number. The platoon symbol was repeated again around the cupola side and front, though it does not appear to have extended around the rear in the case of the M1 medium tank. The regimental number was carried on a disc, probably in red. The regimental crest was painted on the turret side behind the brass Infantry plaque. The vehicle registration number, U.S.A. W-3.0.255, was painted on the hull side.

1

2

The M2A4 light tank design reflected the lessons of the Spanish Civil War, pushing American tank design towards higher levels of armor protection and the use of a 37mm gun instead of the previous machine guns. This M2A4 of the 1st Armored Regiment was taking part in the Third Army maneuvers in Castor, Louisiana, on September 11, 1941. The red cloth wrapped around the turret indicated that it belonged to the Red Army.

in command tanks, and a switch from AM to FM radios. The pilot M2A4 was delivered for trials to APG in the spring of 1939. A committee examining the pilot recommended several changes. The committee was concerned that the long tube of the M6 37mm gun might lead to damage when traveling through wooded areas since it projected beyond the bow, so the M5 37mm gun adopted for tanks was shortened by 5in from the towed Infantry antitank gun. This reduced penetration at 500 yards from 53mm to 50mm.

By the time the M2A4 light tank was ready for production in May 1940, war had broken out in Europe. The US government recognized that its isolationist foreign policy was likely to be challenged, and with it, the need for a substantially enlarged and modernized US Army. As a result, a decision was made to shift tank production from RIA to larger commercial plants to permit a surge in production if war broke out. As a result, M2A4 light tank production began at a large railroad manufacturer, American Car & Foundry, in Berwick, Pennsylvania in May 1940. A total of 325 were manufactured in 1940 and four in January–February 1941 for a sum of 329. The Baldwin Locomotive Works was given a contract for an "educational batch" of 36 tanks, since it was presumed it would be building future light tanks. These were manufactured in February–March 1941, bringing total M2A4 light tank production to 365 tanks. In November 1940, Ordnance recommended that the shorter M5 tank gun be replaced by the M6 37mm tank gun that had the same barrel as the towed Infantry tank gun. Although this was approved prior to the end of M2A4 production, this series was only fitted with the M5 gun. Production of the M2A4 was relatively short-lived as in June 1940, Ordnance recommended that the armor basis be increased from 1in to 1.5in. This was approved in July 1940, leading to the M3 light tank.[4]

4   Steven J. Zaloga, New Vanguard 33: *M3 & M5 Stuart Light Tank 1940–45* (Osprey, 1999).

The Cavalry reluctantly parted with their horses. This shows a column from A Troop, 9th Cavalry being passed by a M2A4 light tank of the 67th Armored Regiment during the September 1941 GHQ maneuvers in Louisiana. The "M" painted on the M2A4 sponson indicates it was serving as a medium tank in the exercise due to the shortage of actual medium tanks.

THE M2 MEDIUM TANK

The T4 medium tank program was short-lived due to the unpopular front-engine configuration. One of the RIA designers, Capt George Rarey, proposed a new medium tank in April 1934 that combined both a barbette and a turret, mounted on a Christie-type chassis such as the T4. The barbette had four machine guns on the superstructure corners in rotor mounts with a 37mm gun in a small turret on top of this. The Ordnance Committee recommended the start of the new T5 medium tank in May 1936. The design followed Rarey's basic concept, but the chassis was an enlarged version of the existing light tank design, using three of the Knox vertical volute bogies per side instead of two. The profusion of machine guns reached ludicrous levels with the addition of a pair of fixed machine guns in the hull front, and provisions for two more machine guns on the exterior of the turret for antiaircraft use, bringing the total to nine .30cal machine guns. A soft steel pilot of the T5 Phase 1 medium tank reached APG for trials in February 1938. Ordnance officers had been advocating the use of a 75mm gun in medium tanks since the mid-1930s, and previous medium tank designs already had incorporated 47 or 57mm guns. The decision against the use of a more powerful gun was due to the Chief of Infantry, Maj Gen George Lynch, who had declared that a weapon as powerful as a 75mm was "needless." Another odd concept incorporated into this tank was the provision of defector plates on the rear corners that would permit the aft machine guns to deflect their bullet stream into trenches below the tank.

This shows one of the machine gunners attempting to use the awkwardly mounted external .30cal turret machine gun on a M2 medium tank of the HQ Company, 67th Infantry Regiment (Medium Tanks), during the Third Army maneuvers at Fort Benning in May 1940.

The Phase I tank was designed to remain under 15 tons due to Corps of Engineer pressure, so the armor was a maximum of 1in (25mm). With reports from the Spanish Civil War becoming available, the designers at RIA received approval from Ordnance to increase the armor to 1.25in (32mm) with a 20-ton limit. This was incorporated into the next Phase 3 pilot; Phase 2 was only a design study. This pilot arrived at APG in November 1938. To provide the T5 with more firepower, the T5E2 was constructed with a 75mm pack howitzer in the right sponson, inspired by the French Char B1 tank. To avoid conflict with the Chief of Infantry's office, the T5E2 was officially labeled as a "gun motor carriage," implying a field artillery weapon. A small turret was fitted included in the design for an optical range-finder. Although stillborn due to Infantry resistance, this would serve as the basis for the later M3 medium tank.

The production version of the T5, the M2 medium tank, retained some features of the Phase 1 such as the symmetric front hull, but used the thicker armor of the Phase 3. Production of 18 M2 tanks was funded in FY39 with production starting at RIA. Although a further 54 tanks were scheduled for FY40, the design had obvious shortcomings. Work on the improved M2A1 began in the summer of 1939. The hull remained much the same but the armor was increased from 1.25in to 1.5in (32–38mm), and a more powerful

The M2A1 medium tank introduced a new turret with vertical sides. A mock attack by A Company, 69th Armored Regiment (Medium), 1st Armored Division in Castor, Louisiana, during the Third Army maneuvers on September 11, 1941 overruns a towed 75mm antitank gun.

version of the R-975 radial engine was used, boosting horsepower from 346 to 400hp. The most noticeable change was the turret, which shifted from angled to vertical sides to increase the internal volume. The testing was straightforward, and the M2A1 was substituted for the M2 in the FY40. However, the Army realized that RIA could not cope with the likely increase in medium tank production, and so Chrysler Corporation was brought in to construct a new tank arsenal in Detroit with the M2A1 as its first product. An August 1940 contract called for the delivery of 1,000 M2A1 tanks by 15 September 1941.

The M2 and M2A1 medium tanks were the most embarrassing and ill-conceived American tanks of the 1930s. Aside from the excessive machine guns, they offered roughly the same level of armor and firepower available on the later light tanks, such as the M2A4, in a much larger and clumsier design. The disparity between the size of this tank and its puny main armament was apparent to the testing team at APG. In their June 1940 report, they recommended it be armed with a 75mm gun or howitzer, a type of recommendation usually outside the purview of the testing organizations. Only a fraction of the machine guns could be used at one time. Of the five-man crew, the driver operated the two fixed machine guns, the two-man turret crew operated the coaxial machine gun and the six remaining machine guns were operated by the two-man machine-gun crew inside the hull. The four rotor-mounted guns in the barbette were sighted through a telescopic sight with no periscope, so the machine gunners had poor situational awareness and would have needed direction from the other crew members. The antiaircraft machine guns stowed on the turret were an even more dubious idea. Although they could be fired from the turret, the awkward location and mounting made it virtually impossible to hit an enemy aircraft. The alternative was for the two hull gunners to stand up in the two hull roof hatches and employ the machine guns from the simple socket mounts fitted to the roof.

In the wake of the lightning German victory in Poland, on October 17, 1939 the chiefs of Infantry and Cavalry, Maj Gen George Lynch and John Herr, met to discuss the possible organization of the first US armored divisions. Lynch had extremely restricted views of the value of tanks, feeling that they were only useful in supporting the Infantry by destroying enemy machine-gun nests. He deferred to the Cavalry to lobby for deeper mechanization and suggested that all tanks under 10 tons go to the mechanized Cavalry, and that only the tanks over 10 tons, namely the M2 and M2A1 medium tanks, would remain with the Infantry. The stunning defeat of France in the summer of 1940 swept away the intransigence of the conservative branch chiefs, and led to the formation of a new mechanized arm under the leadership of one of the maverick Cavalry commanders, Gen Adna Chaffee.

The formation of the Armored Force on July 10, 1940 sealed the fate of the M2A1 medium tank. Chaffee and his staff had been studying the lessons

The T5E2 gun motor carriage was armed with a 75mm pack howitzer in the right sponson. The turret contained an optical range-finder and a .30cal machine gun. This configuration served as the basis for the next step in the evolution of the M2 medium tank family, the M3 medium tank.

of the battle of France and had noted the German use of a 75mm gun on their PzKpfw IV medium tank; likewise the French Char B1 bis was armed with a 75mm gun. With the Chief of Infantry no longer interfering with tank decisions, Chaffee held a meeting with Ordnance in August 1940 and insisted that medium tanks be armed with a 75mm gun. As a result, the August 15, 1940 contract with Chrysler for 1,000 M2A1 tanks was canceled two weeks later to await a new medium tank design. This was the M3 medium tank, which retained a 37mm gun in the turret but placed a 75mm gun in the hull, similar to the T5E2 configuration. RIA was instructed to build 126 M2A1 medium tanks to satisfy short-term training needs, but production was cut short in August 1941 once Chrysler reached a monthly production rate of 80 new M3 medium tanks. In the event, only six M2A1 tanks were built in 1940 and 88 in 1941, for a total of 94.

MARINE CORPS TANKS

Christie attempted to interest the US Marine Corps in several of his amphibious tank designs, but in the event none were acquired. The Marine Corps formed its first light tank platoon in 1923 using eight Six-Ton tanks M1917 obtained from the Army. In 1928, the platoon was deployed to the Marine garrison in Tientsin, China. In the early 1930s, the Marines began to search for a very light tank that could be deployed from a small landing craft. They began acquiring a platoon of Marmon-Herrington CTL-3 in 1935, and another platoon of the improved CTL-3A in 1939.[5] In the turbulent years before the outbreak of World War II, they acquired a handful of other Marmon-Herrington tanks. In the summer of 1940, the Marine Corps requested the transfer of 36 of the new M3 light tanks from the Army, receiving the M2A4 light tank instead. These were the only M2A4 known to have seen combat in World War II, serving with the Marine 1st Tank Battalion on Guadalcanal in August 1942.

5   For more details of the early Marine AFV programs, see Steven J. Zaloga, New Vanguard 186: *US Marine Corps Tanks of World War II* (Osprey, 2012).

A pair of US Marine Corps CTL-3As charge a machine-gun nest during maneuvers at Quantico, Virginia, on August 22, 1941.

EXPORT TANKS

American policy on weapons export was based on an April 23, 1923 decision by President Warren Harding's administration to limit the War Department from selling weapons abroad, based on the popular myth that "merchants of death" had been responsible for pushing the United States into World War I. The War Department revoked the Harding arms sale policy on January 10, 1930 in the hopes that arms export might encourage the growth of an American arms industry. Aside from the Christie and Cunningham sales mentioned earlier, the most significant exporter was the Marmon-Herrington Car Company. The firm designed several light export tanks and sold a few of the CTVL (Combat Tank, Very Light) to Mexico. In 1940, the Royal Netherlands Indies Army approached Marmon-Herrington to purchase a large number of trucks and tanks. In the event, only about a dozen of the CTLS-4TA light tanks were delivered in 1941 prior to the Japanese invasion.

In the early 1930s, the Caterpillar Tractor Company in Peoria was approached by several foreign governments for the sale of tractors for military use. Afghanistan requested the design of an armored body that could be fitted to the Caterpillar Diesel 40 tractor, and ordered nine

G **M2A4 LIGHT TANK, H COMPANY, 66TH ARMORED REGIMENT, 2ND ARMORED DIVISION, FORT BENNING, GEORGIA, 1940**

The new 2nd Armored Division absorbed the Infantry tank regiments stationed at Fort Benning. The tank units in the division adopted colored bands painted around the base of the turret: red (66th Armored); white (67th Armored); blue (68th Armored); and yellow (2nd Reconnaissance Battalion). The 2nd Armored Division also adopted a roundel for air recognition carried on the turret roof and on the turret rear. The colors were the reverse of the US Army Air Force insignia. The armored regiments generally used prominent white letters/numbers to identify the company and individual vehicle. The registration numbers here are still white; blue drab was adopted after November 1940. The M2A4 registration numbers began around 30463 (aside from pilots) and ran beyond 30975; the Baldwin-built tanks were in the 307050-307070 range.

A line of Marmon-Herrington CTLS-4TAC light tanks from the order for the Dutch East Indies. Only about a dozen of the 452 ordered were delivered prior to the Japanese invasion, and the rest ended up with the Australian and US armies.

tractor tanks and three tank bodies. The armor plate was manufactured by the Henry Disston Saw Works near Philadelphia, which also conducted the final assembly. The tanks were armed with a 37mm gun M1916 in the turret and a .30cal machine gun in a ball mount in the hull front. These were delivered in 1935, and due to publicity, four more were ordered by China in 1936 though never delivered. Several other countries examined the type including Canada.

To expedite training until modern tanks became available, in 1940 the United States sold Canada 236 Six-Ton tanks M1917 at scrap value.

Several of the dozen Caterpillar-Disston tractor tanks delivered to Afghanistan in 1935 survived well into the 1990s. At some point, they were rearmed with a Soviet 14.5mm KPVT heavy machine gun in place of the 37mm gun, and with a 12.7mm DShK in place of the .30cal hull machine gun. This particular example was on display at the Afghan army museum in the 1980s. (Wojciech Luczak)

Production of US Tanks and Combat Cars 1931–40

	31	32	33	34	35	36	37	38	39	40
Combat Cars										
T1	-	4	-	-	-	-	-	-	-	-
M1	-	-	-	-	-	33	23	30	-	-
M1A1, M1E1	-	-	-	-	-	-	3	31	-	-
M2	-	-	-	-	-	-	-	-	-	34
T2, T4, T5, T7	1	-	-	2	-	-	1	-	-	-
Light Tanks										
M2A1	-	-	-	1	-	9	-	-	-	-
M2A2	-	-	-	-	-	10	154	74	-	-
M2A3	-	-	-	-	-	-	-	73	-	-
M2A4	-	-	-	-	-	-	-	-	-	325
Medium Tanks										
T3, T3E1	-	-	3	-	-	-	-	-	-	-
T3E2	-	-	-	5	-	-	-	-	-	-
T4 (M1), T4E1	-	-	-	-	-	10	9	-	-	-
T5, M2, M2A1	-	-	-	-	-	-	-	2	18	6
Total	1	4	3	8	-	62	190	210	18	365

IN RETROSPECT

On the verge of its entry into World War II in December 1941, the US Army was well under way to a major expansion of its armored force. From an equipment standpoint, it had a sound light tank design in the form of the M2A4/M3 light tanks, and a mediocre medium tank in the form of its new M3 medium tank. This later deficiency was rectified when the M3 medium tank evolved into the M4A1 medium tank in early 1942. The weakness of US medium tank design was largely due to the peculiarities of prewar US Army organization. In spite of parsimonious budgets, there was the needless waste of two parallel and duplicated lines of light tanks for the Cavalry and Infantry branches. Medium tanks were beyond the Cavalry's budget, while at the same time the Infantry branch neglected medium tanks, since its leadership in the late 1930s had an extremely narrow view of the roles and missions of tanks on the modern battlefield.

In spite of these organizational problems, the interwar tank developments provided the US Armored Force with a sound technical foundation. The many small innovations of Harry Knox – vertical volute suspension, rubber block tracks, incorporation of aircraft engines into tanks – all helped to shape an American tank tradition that placed great emphasis on tank durability. RIA's contribution was not the only component of the success of American tanks in World War II. It was amplified by the 1939 decision to shift from the artisanal construction at RIA to mass industrial production at America's many automotive and railroad factories. This enhanced the durability of the Knox designs due to the quality-control process in the American transportation industry. Tank durability transformed tank warfare and made the tank a decisive weapon on the contemporary battlefield. World War I tanks were useful as siege weapons to break an enemy's defensive line, but they were laborious to deploy and not robust enough to last more than a day or two of fighting. World War II American tanks, more so than any other combatant's tanks in that conflict, were durable enough to operate for thousands of miles and months of combat action without major mechanical breakdowns, making mobile mechanized combat a reality.

FURTHER READING

This book was prepared using a variety of primary and secondary sources. The National Archives and Records Administration (NARA II) in College Park, Maryland, houses most federal documents. Record Group 156 contains the documents of the Chief of Ordnance, and I examined a variety of files including the weekly minutes of meetings of the Technical Staff of the Ordnance Committee, later called the Ordnance Committee Meeting (OCM). Record Group 165 contains the documents of the Military Intelligence Division, which includes some interesting files on tank exports related to the Christie affair. The Library of Congress has George S. Patton's personal papers, which contain a small file on Patton's involvement in the Christie affair. Another useful source is the printed transcripts of the hearings of the Subcommittee of the House Committee on Appropriations for the annual War Department Appropriation Bill. An interesting source of information on the tank design staff at Rock Island Arsenal is the records Patent Office, which help provide some idea of the contributions of various staff members, otherwise lacking in published accounts.

There is an extensive array of published material on US Army mechanization, but most tends to focus on the contentious issues of Army doctrine in the interwar years leading up to the formation of the Armored Force in 1940; there is far less coverage of the technical aspects. The Hunnicutt volumes on US tanks have some coverage of pre-World War II tank development, but these sections are less detailed than the World War II sections, as their titles imply.

Articles

Benson, C. C., "The New Christie Model 1940," *Coast Artillery Journal*, Vol. 71, No. 3 (September 1929), pp.199–207, also in *Army Ordnance*, Vol. X, No. 56 (1929), pp.114–16.

Bogart, Charles, "Major General George Lynch and the Tank 1936–1941," *AFV News*, Vol. 38, No. 3 (Sep–Dec 2003), pp.14–17.

Freeland, W. E., "The Automatic Land Cruiser: Part Played by American Company in Developing the Tanks of the French Battlefield," *The Iron Age*, September 28, 1918, pp.694–95.

Gaare, Dennis, "Edwin Wheelock and the 'Skeleton Tank,'" *Armor*, January–February 2002, pp.35–38.

Grow, Robert, "The Ten Lean Years: From the Mechanized Force (1930) to the Armored Force (1940)," *Armor*, 4 parts: Jan–Feb 1987, Mar–Apr 1987, May–Jun 1987, Jul–Aug 1987.

Hofmann, George, "A Yankee Inventor and the Military Establishment: The Christie Tank Controversy," *Military Affairs*, February 1975, pp.12–18.

Hofmann, George, "The Troubled History of the Christie Tank," *Army*, May 1986, pp.55–65.

Icks, Robert, "Steam Power for Tanks," *AFV G-2*, Vol. 5, No. 4 (1975), pp.6–12.

Lobdell, Jared, "A Civil War Tank at Vicksburg," *Journal of Mississippi History*, Vol. 25, No. 4 (1963), pp.279–83.

Manderfeld, B., "Evidence Accumulates: Was Former Winonan Battle Tank Inventor?," *Winona Sunday News*, 22 August 1971, p.8.

Nenninger, Timothy, "The Development of American Armor 1917–40: The World War I Experience," *Armor*, Jan–Feb 1969, pp.46–49.

Nenninger, Timothy, "The Development of American Armor 1917–40: The Tank Corps Reorganized," *Armor*, Mar–Apr 1969, pp.34–38.

Nenninger, Timothy, "The Development of American Armor 1917–40: The Experimental Mechanized Forces," *Armor*, May–June 1969, pp.33–39.

Dissertations

Cameron, Robert, "Americanizing the Tank: US Army Administration and Mechanized Development within the Army 1917–1943," Temple University (1994).

Cowin, Scott, "Designing US Tanks in the Interwar Period 1918–1941: The Innovations and Tribulations of J. Walter Christie," Stephen Austin State University (1999).

Books

Alexander, Jack, *Briefly Famous: The 1917 Caterpillar G-9 Tank* (Lulu, 2015).

Cameron, Robert, *Mobility, Shock, and Firepower: The Emergence of the US Army's Armor Branch 1917–1945* (Center of Military History, 2008).

Chamberlain, Peter, and Chris Ellis, *Armour in Profile: Tank Mark VIII The International* (Profile Publications, 1967).

Chamberlain, Peter, *Armour in Profile: T.3 Christie* (Profile Publications, 1967).

Christie, J. Edward, *Steel Steeds Christie* (Sunflower University Press, 1985).

Crowell, Benedict, *America's Munitions 1917–1918* (Washington, DC: Office of the Secretary of War, 1919).

Estes, Kenneth, *Marines under Armor: The Marine Corps and the AFV 1916–2000* (Naval Institute, 2000).

Gillie, Mildred, *Forging the Thunderbolt: A History of the Development of the Armored Force* (Harrisburg: Military Service Publishing, 1947).

Hofmann, George, et al., *Camp Colt to Desert Storm: The History of the US Armored Force* (University Press of Kentucky, 1999).

Hofmann, George, *Through Mobility We Conquer: The Mechanization of the US Cavalry* (University Press of Kentucky, 2006).

Hunnicutt, Richard, *Firepower: A History of the American Heavy Tank* (Novato: Presidio, 1998).

Hunnicutt, Richard, *Stuart: A History of the American Light Tank* (Novato: Presidio, 1992).

Hunnicutt, Richard, *Sherman: A History of the American Medium Tank* (Belmont: Taurus, 1978).

Johnson, David, *Fast Tanks and Heavy Bombers: Innovation in the US Army 1917–1945* (Cornell University, 1998).

Lemons, Charles, *Organization and Markings of the United States Armored Units 1918–1941* (Atglen: Schiffer, 2004).

Morton, Matthew, *Men on Iron Ponies: The Death and Re-Birth of the Modern US Cavalry* (Northern Illinois University, 2009).

Nothstein, Ira, et al., *A History of Rock Island Arsenal, Vol. 2: 1898–1940* (Rock Island Arsenal, 1965).

Wilson, Dale, *Treat 'em Rough! The Birth of American Armor 1917–20* (Novato: Presidio, 1989).

INDEX